The Journey:

Life Perspectives from the Eyes of Hunter Nixon

Hunter Nixon

Copyright © 2014 Hunter Nixon
All rights reserved.
ISBN: 1503205614
ISBN-13: 978-1503205611 (Hunter Nixon)

DEDICATION

This book is dedicated to the beautiful life of its author: Hunter Nixon, as well as his terrific parents, Bruce and Kathy.

Hunter, you chose to see the best in others and wanted nothing more than the very best for your friends and family, often at your own expense. If you ever found out that someone needed help, you were there for that person. Your perspective on life and personable nature is valued by all and remains with us to this day. More than anything, you were a genuinely nice guy with a heart that could barely fit inside of your chest. There are not many folks quite like you in the world.

From the outside looking in, it was probably even hard for people to tell your friends from those who were strangers to you. That's the kind of inviting spirit that you projected 24-7 in your conversations with others. People have even been known to think of themselves as "cooler" just by their association with you.

You left something of yours with a friend down here a couple of years back along with this note:

"I just wrote this for one of my buddies… I think whole cultures can move in this same fashion I'm describing here, just as cultures can move in the wrong direction…I've updated it and added some concepts; maybe it will be a book one day…Dude, every day I'm getting more and more insightful realizations and building my brain around them. I think there might be something seriously significant going on here. I don't know what is going to happen, but all I know is that it makes me want to learn and think more and more every day. My habits are changing; I'm seeing through a lot of my faults. I'm helping others. I know this is the start of something crazy…I know you will be involved in whatever is going on here when the time is right. For now I think we both have work to do."

Hunter, we thank you for your beautiful words. The time is right. Here is your book:

CONTENTS

Chapter 1: An Introduction

Chapter 2: Think About Where You're Going

Chapter 3: Mind Mapping

Chapter 4: Stay Disciplined

Chapter 5: A Call to Action for My Friends

Chapter 1: An Introduction

These are some of my recommended instructions and guidelines for what I call "The Journey." First, I want to touch on my way of viewing all new information that I am taking in and trying to process:

First, I'm finding that it is best to relate everything new you learn to what you already know. You may do so by looking at the knowledge you acquire in terms of being part of your collective knowledge database rather than separating this knowledge into compartments. The reason for this is that if you don't do this you may pull up a thought or situation and it could be very closely related to something you already know, but you still could never "make the connection" in your brain that the two are even similar.

Everything is connected, so your brain should be too. As the famous quote goes: "It's better to travel well than to arrive." The Journey is your life, and your *true* life will only be lived while you are moving. You must be moving to go on any journey, therefore, if you are not moving you are not going on any journeys.

In order to move, you must have motivation; it is your fuel, whether it is in the form of inspiration, desperation, desire, fear, or something else. In my opinion, it's best to remind yourself that you are on a journey every day, so you can stay focused and keep burning desires inside of you that will serve as your fuel.

Like any long journey, the long-term motivation is what keeps you going: This requires persistent energy focused in one direction. If the motivation is simply geared toward healthy progress, learning, and implementation, then everything else will naturally follow.

In my opinion, the most effective way to build motivation so you always have a full fuel tank is through the principles of auto-suggestion (There is more to be found on this subject by way of a simple Google search). I also recommend reading all of "Think and Grow Rich" by Napoleon Hill. Another good book to start with is "Awaken the Giant Within" by Tony Robbins. I have also found quick motivation through Steve Pavlina's blog site.

Chapter 2: Think About Where You're Going

The second part of The Journey requires one to be conscious of WHERE he or she is moving, so one does not get stuck moving in circles. Wandering off your path and getting stuck moving in circles is a waste of your time and energy. Things like: doing drugs, drinking, or binding oneself to other generally bad habits are examples of walking in circles on The Journey.

I have also found that emphasizing the desire to remember all the bad times you would like to forget will help one to remember natural characteristics of what it looks like to walk in circles. Walking a trail that was unpleasant can be forgotten on purpose, which provides the comfort of not having to remember a former problem. But there is a downside to this: Not being able to remember what the first few steps down the wrong trail look like. If you forget your past completely, you may be in too deep before you know it and get stuck walking in circles again before you find the energy to break free.

How and where you move makes all the difference, and this is controlled by mastering the relationship between your conscious and subconscious mind. Over time you will be able to visualize how fast you are moving mentally and you will know whether or not you are going in the right direction. With that being said, it is still very possible to get stuck in circles, especially early on before you are an experienced trailblazer. In the words of Ben Franklin: "All of mankind is divided into three classes: those that are immovable, those that are movable and those that move." That quote applies in countless ways and is worth some thought.

Find the best way to travel for yourself. Just like your first day of college, or the first time you visit Europe, you will not really know exactly what to expect on The Journey. You may have a slight glimpse of what's in store, but there is no way to be sure, so it's better to prepare for anything than to predict something. As you move along you will find things among your travels that you want to keep, whether it be insights on yourself, insights on others, concepts for changing your outlook on life, etc. Whatever the insights and concepts are, if you place them down and leave them somewhere, it's possible to forget where you placed them. This is why you add new information to yourself while taking mental inventory of what you already know, so that new knowledge is tied back to something familiar in your mind. (Neurologically, this actually adds more connections so that if one connection fails, during a time in which you need it, others remain. The same thing occurs if you want to cut rope into two pieces. It would be a lot more difficult to do this if the rope were in the form of a net).

The same can also be said about negative thought processes and mindsets. They can be picked up looking seemingly harmless, but you can actually carry them with great burden without even realizing that they are the reason you feel so negative.

Chapter 3: Mind Mapping

In The Journey, there will be moments of clarity. For instance, say your journey is in a hypothetical forest and you need to get out of it. You can climb a tree to see where you need to go, but unless you take good note of what you see while you are up there, you could soon forget what once seemed clear when you go back down to the forest to continue walking.

There are many ways to take note and map your journey (I would suggest writing in a journal, iPhone, laptop, etc.). You will find that some ways are better than others, but the way you decide to map your journey is ultimately up to you.

Chapter 4: Stay Disciplined

Something else to remember on The Journey is to value your self-discipline! If you find something and say to yourself: "Wow, imagine if I put this concept to use. I could really go far." Well, how about you don't just imagine if you did and actually do it instead?

You may say something like: "Man, I should go to the gym, but I don't really feel like it." This is acceptable on occasion, but when it's constant, there is an obvious motivational issue that needs to be addressed. If this is the case, you need to reprogram you subconscious to achieving your conscious priorities.

Motivation dictates everything you do. You are a creator, so motivation uses whatever ideas you create and feed your thought energy into in order to create something real. This means that if you feed the idea of valuing time spent sitting on your ass enough, it can surely overpower any idea you have of doing anything else productive. (Sitting by the way is not a necessary human state beyond getting the sufficient rest needed to function).

As grown adults, we create our circumstances; as a child, your parents created them for you. Be fully aware of the circumstances you create for yourself. Understanding that people create circumstantial illusions of importance in every aspect of their lives and being able to differentiate the illusions from the truth are a big deal (For more info on this, Google Steve Pavlina's ideas on the abuse of power).

Emotions in your life that you have to deal with are created by YOU at some point or another. When you create an idea, it is like an empty vessel that has the capability of holding thought energy. You can feed an idea with either positive or negative energy, which in turn will feed your emotions.

The more thought energy you invest into an idea, the deeper it will affect you on an emotional level (This is why a sports fanatic may cry over the super bowl; he invested enough thought energy for the outcome of that idea to release all of that thought energy as negative or positive emotion at the drop of a hat based on his team's success or failure).

I find it best to visualize my emotions as balls of energy (This took a while to get an accurate mental depiction of). I can then see better what I invest my emotions into. Remember, emotions are what drive us, and to master them takes time. Mastering emotions requires significant amounts of thought energy. It is also critical to invest our emotion into the right ideas.

Chapter 5: A Call to Action for My Friends

What The Journey boils down to is the fact that you can do ANYTHING you want. You can be a genius if you choose. Do you want it?

We are creators, but to succeed you must create certainty. If you "don't know" what you want that's because you decided to create the mental state of you not knowing, and until you create a better option, you will continue not to know. So what the hell are you waiting for?

ABOUT THE AUTHOR

Hunter Nixon was a blessing to all. He was a son, grandson, a nephew, a blood brother, a fraternity brother, a friend, a cousin, a boyfriend, and the friendliest stranger anyone could ever meet.

Few men in this world have ever enjoyed the favor of a man like Hunter amongst such a wide variety of circles. His perspective on life was deep. His demeanor was contagious, causing everyone to love him.

One thing is for sure: If you were around Hunter, you were smiling. Hunter's legacy lives on in the hearts of all who know and love him. He has made a real difference in this world and his words will continue to inspire others.

Remembering Hunter:

Rip hunter u were Like a little brother I am glad we got to talk more and u called me a lot for advice u will be missed I will never forget all the times at the lake and watching u grow up since u were a baby love and miss u buddy.
–Clint Machamer

RIP Hunter Nixon. You left too soon my friend. My thoughts and prayers are with your family during this hard time.
May the road rise up to meet you.
May the wind be always at your back.
May the sun shine warm upon your face;
the rains fall soft upon your fields and until we meet again, may God hold you in the palm of His hand.
-Brendan DeKemper

It still does seem real. You always have been a genuine fun soul. Rest in peace knowing you've brought joy to everyone you've come across in this world. You are and will continue to be missed by all who loved you Hunter Nixon.
-Michelle DiPietro

Hunter Nixon was one of the most kind people I have ever met, such a big heart.
-Ryan Lorenzetti

It was such an honor to have met you Hunter. Rest easy sweet boy.
-Remy Michelle

My heart is so heavy, tears come to my eyes every time I think of you, You were always a good friend to Samantha and Nick and like a son to Steve and I. We have so many fond memories of you. My heart hurts for your Mom, Dad, family, girlfriend and of course your many friends. I know you had many – you were just that kind of guy. You had such an impact on so many, including our family. It really wasn't all that long ago that you were part of our daily lives but even when you and Sam were no longer a couple you were still very dear to our family. You and Sam shared wonderful memories of a first love. You had a deep friendship and bond for one another and I know you both only wanted the best for each other. Sam and our family will miss so much about you. Our family will forever hold a special place in our hearts for you. Thank you Hunter, for so many wonderful memories and for sharing your heart and spirit with us.
Much Love Always and Forever.
-The Doris Family

I am in shock. It feels like yesterday He came down to Statesboro to visit with Wesley when I was in school there. We took him to Dingus MaGees for his first time and introduced him to SAE. I remember how excited he was to get a bid and he called me to tell me. I visited Statesboro for homecoming a few years later and visited the chapter, I will always remember how proud of him I was when I saw the love his brothers had for him. I will forever be grateful for having met Hunter and to be able to call him Brother. Rest in peace little brother.
-Nick Parke

I first met Hunter at GAC but ended up sitting by him at Northview my short stint there Senior year. I had just been through prob. the hardest experience I have ever had to deal with to date. I was extremely self-conscious of what others thought of me and had a very low opinion of myself unfortunately. Truthfully at the time I had one friend, my boyfriend at the time. On my first day, I was terrified to be sitting next to him bc i knew he had heard everything about me...however he never once judged me. He made me laugh and smile and unlike every other person he actually asked me what had happened instead of making assumptions and talking bad about an experience no one can fathom until it happens to you... He told me it was okay and he was sorry and told me he was my friend and not to worry what other people thought He reassured me I was in a new school and was going to have a great school year, and I didn't need to think about the previous school and people there, if they were true friends they would still be there. He was working at Publix by my apartment and at school- after school he was always making me smile and just being a friend. He never talked behind my back. He made me feel comfortable to make new friends and he invited me to parties and he treated me with unconditional friendship. I can never repay him for that.
-Kelsey Nash

Hunter for the short time that I've known you, I've always admired your energetic friendly character and your genuine love for life. The world needs more people like you. It pains me that you're gone because I AM proud to call you my friend. My thoughts and prayers go out to your friends and family...........Good bye for now.
-Brandon Knowles

I'm honored to hold Hunter in my Pride. I'm eternally grateful for the conversations & adventures we've shared. Acknowledging Hunter's thirst for Knowledge and Understanding will always sit well with me. I have always admired his tactful & dedicated approach for other's understanding. A random summer at the Lodge comes to mind. We had randomly stumbled upon a keyboard (with Tom) and you had immediately started playing Moonlight Sonata (and Adele, with your singing). You were dedicated in having me learn it. Your random talents and teachings will always be good indicators of your modesty. Your egg-in-a-hole was the best of AΩ. When in Rome, we will never forget to check the expiration date of a milk jug again (Chris).
-Mike Redmon

My thoughts are with the Nixon family. Hunter always had a smile on his face, was a fun person to be around but most importantly a good man who knew how to treat his friends and people right. RIP Hunter.
-Austin Hannon

Hunter passed away in a car accident this weekend. It would really mean a lot to me if you could please send some good vibes and prayers to his family and to his loved ones. Hunter was a great friend and will be missed by a lot of people, including me.
Life is short.... Way too short.
-John Andrew Smoltz

Feeling grateful to have had Hunter in my life even if it was only for a short while. He was so unique and had such a caring, nurturing heart, an epic smile and sense of humor that could turn anyone's bad day around. you are missed already.
-Patrick Swindall

Hunter I am so thankful I got to spend time with you in your last hours. How warm and loving you were when I was sad. You came into the apt bringing Andie and I flowers, offered me a sip of your milkshake, and gave me a hug to make me feel better. You really do give the best hugs much love Hunter.
-Shauna Powers

Hunter I am so grateful to have known you. You touched so many lives, you will be greatly missed. My prayers are with the Nixon family during this difficult time.
-Alyssa Susanne

Once you think life is right where you want it, God throws you a curve ball, rest easy Hunte, my oldest best friend!
-Jackson Petusky

You will be missed my friend, but we will always have these memories.
-Jay Curnin Jr.

Hunter the world is a lesser place without you I may have only spent a small amount of time with you but I know you were a very special person and I am glad to have known you. My love and prayers are with your family.
-Katy Glover

There's no way to convey my gratitude for your friendship, or my thanks for the memories I am lucky to have shared. I am shocked to hear that you are gone, the world is shy another great soul. Save me a seat at the ball game, pal.
-Lucas Macy

My cousin is gone I will miss him every day. I love you Hunter.
-Christine Wearing

Hunter I cannot believe this ... It's hard for words over Facebook .. Does not do justice . All I can say is you are a great man who influenced all of us .. We will always be there for u . We all will see you soon . Like a Phoenix your greatness will affect all whom you've met. Phi alpha BROTHER.
-Jordan Rossi

Rest in peace Hunter. You were the sweetest guy and always had the most positive outlook on life. You will truly be missed by everyone who had the good fortune of knowing you. My thoughts and prayers are with the Nixon family and the brothers of SAE.
-Emily Ann

RIP Hunter. The world could use a whole lot more people with his heart. Taught me a lot about commitment and accountability. He impacted several peoples lives and will never be forgotten. Much love, my brother.
-Joseph Cook

The world has lost a special person with an amazing spirit with your passing. You made everyone around you a better person, and that is the hallmark of a great friend. I am so thankful to have spent our childhoods together, and for all you taught me. Rest well Hunter.
-Drew Daniels

Rest in peace Hunter. You were an awesome guy my man! Phi alpha brother.
-Emory Huegel

Hunter, you were a great friend to many, It's truly tragic to hear of your passing. You'll be greatly missed but never forgotten.
-Daniel Wright

I never got to say just how much you helped me turn around in college. You were by far, one of the best people I've known in my life and the world won't be the same without you brotha. The way you could turn any bad day around will never be forgotten.
-Alex Berman

I love you bud. I will think about you every day. You were something else man. I don't think I've ever told you how much you have inspired me and will even more now. You're an inspiration to me and so many. You've touched so many lives. You will never be forgotten. Ever. My kids will know your name. I love you so much dude. Things will never be the same.
-Ryan Swindall

It's amazing to see how many lives have been changed by your contagious personality. I am so grateful that even in your afterlife you are bringing us all back together. I wish you could be here to see all the love and support people have for you. I know that nothing would make you happier than to see everyone you love come together to reunite and celebrate your beautiful life!
-Samantha Rose Doris

"The true mind can weather all the lies and illusions without being lost. The true heart can tough the poison of hatred without being harmed. Since beginningless time, darkness thrives in the void, but always yields to purifying light." RIP Hunter, your positive outlook on life will live on through the friends and brothers you have. I will miss talking with you even though I know you are in a better place.
-Anthony Picone

I'm so glad to have had the opportunity to meet this awesome guy, Hunter. May your soul rest in peace. Be the angel to look after your sweet girlfriend, Andie. She's going to need you. Prayers for both families.
-Chelsea Tiller

Rest in peace Hunter. Your fun loving soul will be missed.
-Cassie Eng

Hunter, we had lost touch but we were definitely friends. I had known you since elementary school through high school and after..You were always full of spirit and making everyone around you smile. I'm praying for you and your family. Can't believe you were taken from us this early. All because of a car crash. Rest in peace buddy. I know you're in a better place now.
-Corey O'Brien

Hunter, where do I begin? I've known you for 13 years now and you are by far one of my best friends in this fucked up world. You have the sweetest, most loving Ora, you are so genuine and nurturing, your always there whenever I need you and you have been such an amazing friend throughout these years. The love we've had for each other is unconditional and unforgettable; I really don't even know what to say right now. My heart is broken and a little piece of me died with you yesterday. I don't know why God took you from us so soon and I don't think I'll ever understand but no doubt in mind my you were made a beautiful angel. I know you'll be watching over me and your family everyday with every step we take. One day we'll be reunited but until then I'll continue to pray and love your family and remember all the life changing memories we had together. I love you so much Hunter. May your beautiful soul rest in peace my baby, my Huntie, my best friend. I love you and I'll be seeing you.
-Taylor Corley

It's hard to explain the attitude Hunter had on life, but I think this picture can help. He smiled for no reason, he had a real appreciation for life, and it rubbed off on anyone around him. You were the biggest intellectual I've ever met. You listened to Tony Robbins, and read a new book every week, filling me in on everything you learned. Some of my best college memories are with you brother, and I'm heartbroken that are chapter has come to a close. Watch over us from chapter eternal, Phi Alpha Hunter.
-Chris Moore

At a loss for words... rest in peace, Hunter. You were always a great joy to be around and had such a kindhearted soul. You will be missed my friend. Praying for your family and friends.
-Kat Hill

Hunter, You will be missed dearly. Praying for the Nixon family in this difficult time.
-Deniz Beyhan

Rest in peace hunter. You are truly one of the sweetest guys I've ever known, and I can't believe the few short weeks ago that I ran into you in Buckhead was the last time I will ever see you. I will always cherish the memories I had with you throughout middle and high school, I never did get to thank you for helping me roll my old boyfriends house when he was mean to me. Halie Uzelac, remember that?! Rest easy hunter and prayers to your family.
-Meredith Adrienne

Yesterday the world lost a truly unique and amazing person. Thoughts and prayers go out to all my friends and neighbors coping with the loss of such an incredible guy. Hunter I'll miss you a lot bud, but I know I'll see ya again someday.
-Linley Ann Davis

I ncredibly saddened by this news. You were a genuine friend to many and will be missed by all. It's extremely tragic to see you taken so soon, but I'm sure your looking down on us all from a better place. It was always a joy to be in your company. Rest in peace Hunter.
-Peter Velardi

Hunter, Hunter you were taken to soon. I wish we could go back to the old days and sneak over your back fence to the walmart and play man hunt on the golf course. You will be missed my friend.
-Deano McDonald

Wow! I honestly dont know where to start, I just asked your mum for you on Friday, ;(. You always was a uplifting person, I've truly lost a friend. R.I.P my brother.
-Lavell McKinney

I don't even know where to begin. I will always remember the good times that we had together. You are the most genuine, kind and good hearted friend that I have ever had and ever will have. I will miss you buddy, but I know that you are in a better place now watching down on all of us and making sure that we don't do anything stupid (mainly me). RIP buddy you will be missed, but never forgotten.
-Chris Schauerman

Hunter I know you touched a lot of people's lives, yet another soul gone too soon.
-Danielle Shearer

Hunter was hands down one of the nicest, most genuine people I've ever met. Wasn't blessed to know him extremely well but in the few times we hung out he always made me laugh hysterically or smile, every time I would talk to him, I was a happier person than before, that's what living is truly all about, to make other lives better and to spread positivity and he definitely did that to the fullest. He brought joy to my life each time we crossed paths and for that I must say thank you.
-Kyle Khuri

I'll never forget the times we had. Rest in peace Hunter.
-Jen Gresenz

I am terribly saddened by the tragic loss of my sweet brother Hunter. He was born the year I met Wesley and we have loved watching him grow into the incredible person is. We have such wonderful memories that we will cherish. Thank you for the prayers and please keep them going for my dad and Kathy.
-Heather Nixon DeFoor

I' m at a lost of words. I've been thinking of what to say and words can not describe how I feel right now. I have nothing but awesome memories with you. Never a dull moment with you bud. I'm gonna miss you Hunter; you were a true friend that was always there for me. My thoughts and prayers go out to Kathy and Bruce Nixon.
-Kyle Murphy

Rest in peace Hunter. ou were such a sweet guy! You will be greatly missed! Prayers to your family and close friends!
-Angela Drumheller

Rest in peace Hunter. My thoughts and prayers go out to your family in this hard time. You will be missed greatly and never forgotten.
-Robert Neville

My love and prayers go out to Kathy and Bruce Nixon during this tragic time. Hunter brought joy into so many people's hearts and touched everyone he met. He will be missed and remembered by so many friends and family.
-Sabrina Kuhn

Wow this is shocking... It was great knowing you and playing baseball with you... Rest in peace Hunter.
-Drew Terry

Hunter I don't wanna believe it. I'm so sorry that something like this happened to you. You'll remain forever in my heart, rest in peace sweet boy.
-Jessica Barnes

Prayers and thoughts go out to the brothers of SAE. Hunter you were one of the most optimistic and good spirited people I've ever met and you will be missed buddy.
-Evan Strohofer

Hunter you were loved by so many. I am so thankful to have known you.. You were such a light in so many people's lives and you will always be remembered for that. Keeping you and your family in my prayers. We love you.
-Heidi Uzelac

Hunter I am heartbroken that you're not here anymore. I'm so thankful to have had you in my life. Thank you for being such an amazing man and loyal friend to me and my family for so many years. Thank you for picking me and my brother up for school every morning, making CDs for me, and always having my back. I love you and miss you so much!
-Bess Paddock

You were such a genuine person. You will be truly missed.
-Ally Brophy

RIP to my friend and colleague Hunter, who died in a car accident yesterday at 22 in Atlanta GA. You will be missed but I know you are in a better place now. Your family will be in my prayers.
-Nicolas Palmisano

I'm so sad by the news I received this morning. Hunter, you will be missed by all. You were one of the most positive people I've ever met and don't think I ever saw you without a smile on your face; you were destined to do big things. May the Nixon family, brothers of SAE and all whose lives you touched, find peace in such a loss.
-Hallie Anderson

There aren't words to describe your positive personality and how you've affected people's lives. Such a genuine friend, man. Love you Hunter.
-JR Kaney

I'm so sad to hear this devastating news. It was a blessing to have been able to know you. I will always cherish the memories I have with you. Rest easy.
-Mayce Bishop

My heart weighs heavy this morning. Getting word of my dear friend, Hunter. My thoughts and prayers are with him and his family. It was an honor and a blessing having him in my life, especially this past year -He helped me more than words can explain. I love you, hunter.
-Gadsden Henderson

I'm so sad this morning. I don't even have words to explain how my heart feels. I found out last night that this sweet, loving and kind 23 year old young man was killed Friday in a car accident. It was my pleasure to share just a few moments at the fair with Tonya Gambrell-Thompson and Hunter. Hunter it was my pleasure to share time, laughter, red velvet funnel cakes and super fun pics with you. We loved getting to know you and the laughter and fun we shared with you my sweet friend will always be in our hearts. As a parent myself, I can't imagine the grief his family is experiencing right now. Please keep them in your prayers.
-Dawn Ogburn Brown

Praying for your family and all your friends, Hunter. Your kind heart and bright spirit will truly be missed by all. I am blessed to have known you and will remember you in all the good memories. May you rest in peace.
-Becca Anderson

My thoughts and prayers go out to Hunter, his family, and everyone that was so close to him in the St. Ives Community.
-Eric Matthieson

Hunter you had the biggest heart of anyone I knew, I'm going to miss you brother.
-Mike Jones

Still can't believe the news I received last night. I know God has a plan but sometimes I just don't understand it. Heaven gained an angel. Gone too soon, but never forgotten. Rest in peace my friend.
-Hannah Pendleton

Miss you Hunter thanks for making Drink a Beer by Luke Bryan the first song played as I get in my car after a long night of work... Have been trying to be distracted but it's hard not to sit and wonder why you were taking so early from our lives. Please help us get through this time. I wish you and Ryan Swindall could just be headed to Brookhaven today to have some beers and watch some football. My heart and prayers go out to you Kathy and Bruce. Love you guys!
-Mackenzie Swindall

Hunter you left the Earth way too early. Thank you for the short time we had with you. You were always such a nice young man with such a positive outlook. Heaven gained an angel. Georgette and I send our deepest condolences to your parents,Kathy and Bruce and your whole family. RIP buddy. We'll miss you.
-Peter Binnington

I'll never forget the first time I met you in Statesboro. I dragged Andie to Dingus, and little did I know you two would have a love for each other unlike any other. It really isn't fair how short life is sometimes. Watch over us up there, RIP.
-Cassie King

Just woke up this morning and what popped up was my Hunter had passed away last night. My heart has just sunk I am so upset, Hunter was a Brother of mine. I met Hunter while we was working at Publix together. He schooled me to a lot, we talked about life, love, and the future . Hunter was a true friend of mines, Hunter I will miss you my Brother.
-John Goodwin

Tragedy it is unexpected. Makes no sense. Makes you wish you had done more, said more made that person know what they meant to you.
My beautiful brother only 22 was killed yesterday alone in a car accident.
He was a beautiful person. He was Sweet and kind. A good man. A tender person. I will miss him every day. Things happen unexpectedly let everyone in your life know everyday how much they mean to you. I can't express the heartbreak or emotion or sadness and pain I feel for my parents and sweet Hunter taken too early from this world.
-Natalie Nixon

Hunter, you will forever be remembered. Your joyous attitude and constant enthusiasm towards everyone you encountered will truly be missed. You taught myself and everyone around you that there is always a reason to have a positive outlook on life. The brothers of Georgia Alpha will never forget the everlasting impression you made on us all. Our deepest prayers go out to your family and friends everywhere.
-Dakota Socha

The hardest part of teaching is losing a student, and it doesn't matter how long it has been since that student left my classroom. Love to all of my kids who are stunned by the loss of smart, funny, genuine Hunter.
-Elizabeth Lake

Another soul that God took soon. I love you. I wish things weren't this way. Rest in paradise brother.
-Matt Larre

My heart is extremely heavy right now and I can't even believe it..Hunter, you were the most genuine and sweet boy I've ever had the pleasure of growing up with. You had the biggest heart and you were such a great friend to so many. I'll never forget all times we had in the neighborhood and all the trouble we all got into. There are so many stories I'll never forget. You'll always have a special place in my heart, rest in peace.
-Halie Uzelac

SAE lost a really great, loyal brother this weekend. Rest In Peace Hunter. You were taken way too soon, but I'm thankful for the times we shared. You were a great room mate, brother, and person. My thoughts, prayers, and love go out to Mr. and Mrs. Nixon. I'll see you again someday buddy.
-Bud Burruss

I'm still in complete shock over this. You have one of the most beautiful souls there is. Words cannot explain how lucky I feel to have had all the time I had with you. Beautiful memories like this will stay with me forever!! 9 years ago we decide that 311- "love song" would be our song and it has held true to this day. " however far away I will always love you" even after we broke up we remained the best of friends and I owe so much to you. You were ALWAYS there when I needed you, just a phone call away!! Rest in peace you beautiful soul tell poppy and Bella hello for me!
-Samantha Rose Doris

Hunter, you were always a very positive and loyal friend.
-Tom Clarke

The most painful goodbyes are the ones that are never said and never explained. SAE lost a good brother and a True Gentlemen today. RIP Hunter. You were one of the most positive and outgoing individuals I ever had the privilege to know, and I'm damn proud to call you my brother. Watch over the rest of us buddy. Phi Alpha.
-Richie Wiltfang

Words can't describe the way that I feel right now. You've been a best friend ever since i moved to Atlanta, there for me when no one else was, and always had my back. The world has lost a light but heaven gained one. Rest in peace Hunter, I love you as a brother and always will. Don't have too much fun up there, I'll join you one day to continue our shenanigans. But until then, be easy brother.
-Carter Michael

Hunter, you were such a great guy with a sense of humor that could always put a smile on everyone's face, I know your wonderful spirit is in a better place but you'll be truly missed. RIP buddy thoughts & prayers with the Nixon family.
-Brittany Clark

Where my heart is... Love you baby.

-Andie Strangi

Made in United States
Orlando, FL
19 July 2024